Go Outside!

PLAY
HIDE-AND-SEEK!

By Peter Finn

Gareth Stevens
PUBLISHING

Please visit our website, www.garethstevens.com. For a free color catalog of all our high-quality books, call toll free 1-800-542-2595 or fax 1-877-542-2596.

Library of Congress Cataloging-in-Publication Data

Names: Finn, Peter, 1978- author.
Title: Play hide-and-seek! / Peter Finn.
Description: New York : Gareth Stevens Publishing, 2020. | Series: Go
  outside! | Includes index.
Identifiers: LCCN 2019009909| ISBN 9781538244975 (pbk.) | ISBN 9781538244999
  (library bound) | ISBN 9781538244982 (6 pack)
Subjects: LCSH: Hide-and-seek.
Classification: LCC GV1207 .F56 2020 | DDC 793.4–dc23
LC record available at https://lccn.loc.gov/2019009909

Published in 2020 by
Gareth Stevens Publishing
111 East 14th Street, Suite 349
New York, NY 10003

Editor: Therese Shea
Designer: Sarah Liddell

Photo credits: Cover, pp. 1, 11 Diego Cervo/Shutterstock.com; p. 5 Sergey Novikov/Shutterstock.com; p. 7 wavebreakmedia/Shutterstock.com; pp. 9, 24 (bench) MaraZe/Shutterstock.com; p. 13 iofoto/ Shutterstock.com; p. 15 perfectlab/Shutterstock.com; p. 17 valbar/Shutterstock.com; pp. 19, 24 (bush) Zabolotskikh Sergey/Shutterstock.com; p. 21 XiXinXing/Shutterstock.com; p. 23 Iakov Filimonov/ Shutterstock.com.

Printed in the United States of America

Some of the images in this book illustrate individuals who are models. The depictions do not imply actual situations or events.

CPSIA compliance information: Batch #CW20GS: For further information contact Gareth Stevens, New York, New York at 1-800-542-2595.

Contents

I'm Cam.
I love hide-and-seek!

I ask friends to play with me.

We play in the park.
There are lots
of hiding places.

My friend Dan
will seek first.
He covers his eyes.
He counts to 10.

Everyone runs!
We find a place
to hide.

Kim hides behind
a tree.

Lee hides behind
a bench.

Lily hides in a bush.
Dan finds her!

We play again!

We play hide-and-seek inside, too!
Hide-and-seek is fun!

Words to Know

bench

bush

Index

24